The Heart of It

~

Select Poems
1979-2015

by

James A. Moore

Opti-Mystic Books
2015

Published by
Opti-Mystic Books
P.O. Box 1616
Tonasket, WA. 98855
U.S.A.
www.opti-mysticarts.com

First edition 2015

Printed in the United States of America

James A. Moore; 1958 –
The Heart of It – Select Poems 1979 – 2015

ISBN-13: 978-0692386682
ISBN-10: 0692386688

Cover illustration, "Solo Humpback"
original oil painting by James Moore, 2010

To my parents;

James A. Moore 1921-2002
&
Gennifer H. Moore 1930-2011

Contents

Introduction

Illustrations

Acknowledgments

Although there have been too many people to name who have influenced me in both small and great ways, I'd like to acknowledge the women who have each in their own way made my life meaningful and complete;

Mother: Gennifer Heppell Moore,

Sister: Caroline Moore Anzur

Partners: Maile Wall, Theresa Carel, & Carol Ogilvie,

Daughters: Leneya Ludwick, Rachael Ludwick, & Shae Celeste Moore,

And my father, James Anderson Moore II, who was not only my primary role model, mentor and teacher during my early years, but also my best friend in his later ones.

A special thanks to my dharma sister Cyndy Roomy – for always being there, and for helping edit this collection.

Introduction

I have never considered myself much of a connoisseur of poetry. Although I have been deeply moved by some poems, I frankly have more often found it a difficult form of literature to appreciate. And while I love to write "poetry" I wouldn't presume to call myself a poet. If anything I feel my best and most inspired poetic efforts have been in the naming of climbing routes – what I call my passion as a "two word poet."

Yet I have often enjoyed poets like Lao Tzu, Rumi, Rilke, Yeats, Rexroth, Snyder and Hunter, who embody a romantic, earthy and mystical appreciation for life and living, which whenever I read make me think this is what I feel and know, or at least want to feel and know.

This collection of 36 poems is culled from the past 36 years, the full range of my adult life so far, and represent vivid moments, which even if filtered through strong conceptual layers, have come from the heart. They are listed chronologically to help show the passage of time; time and the inevitable change it brings.

So here we have it; life, death, love, loss and growth... a theme best described as simply living and trying to figure out what this means.

The illustrations accompanying these pages are all original works of art I have either drawn, painted, block printed or carved during this time.

There is also a postscript included of an essay I wrote a couple of years ago about my cat Pluto, poetry if you will, but with lots of words.

The Heart of It

Select Poems
1979-2015

To Claudia

To the friend
who loved in freedom
and danced in joy
who suddenly stopped
and appeared not
willing to return
to pull us together
and away from surfaces
to deep
with mystic rhythms
from above
we celebrate love
and move in unknown
silence.

(In my second year at college I had a friend, Claudia, who was part of a small modern contact-dance group I had joined. I had just spent about a week hanging out a lot with her, having an affair I guess, but one of the heart and not sexual. We were at a Saturday night dance together in her dorm, dancing in the dim light to Neil Young's "Cortez The Killer" when she came up to hug and kiss me and say something like "thank you, I have learned so much this past week." I didn't quite know what she meant, but that was the last thing she said. A minute or so later she simply and peacefully lay down and died. Somehow I knew exactly what had happened as I sat on the floor beside her as the music played on, held her hand and quietly said goodbye. At no time did I think to call for help, or attempt CPR, for she had simply gone. It was never clear what had happened to Claudia. She wasn't a drug user, and was apparently healthy, happy and comfortable when she died. She probably had an aneurism. Somehow I wasn't surprised or upset by her passing, maybe because she had always impressed me as being 'an old soul'.

After the ambulance took her body away I went home, smoked a couple of joints and wrote this poem. A few days later at her memorial service I read it aloud and participated in a short choreographed madrigal dance in her honor. Apparently when it was my turn to do a few solo steps I went into a trance and danced at length in some beautiful way. I have no memory of doing this. It was at a time in my life when I was open and somewhat confused and just beginning to explore what death really is, and in a very vivid way Claudia showed me, took me to the edge and then even across for a moment.)

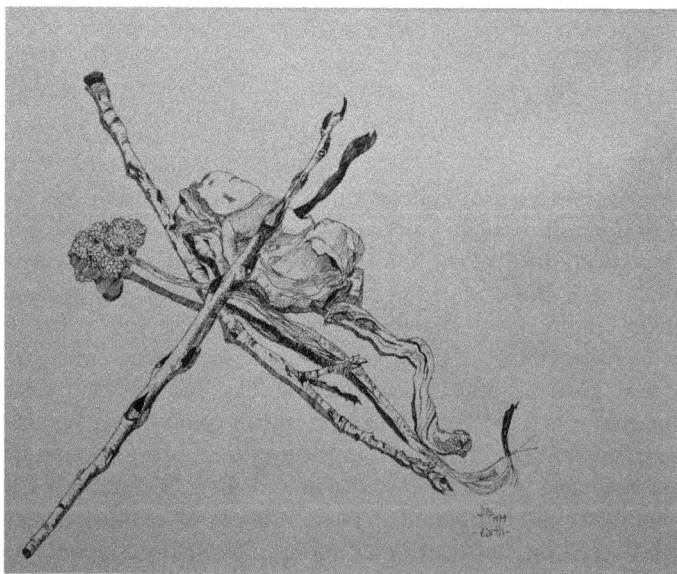

Laughing Vajra

Oh Laughing Vajra
dear kindest father
to whom all life's a play
With words just flashing,
bubbling, dancing
exactly is your way

Oh Laughing Vajra
most patient companion
your words so make me smile
While inside you roar
and outside you wheeze
we devoted learn from your style

Oh Laughing Vajra
strong elder brother
your wisdom floods my mind
As humor drowns me
and I split my sides
your compassion is gentle and kind

(Written after experiencing a roar of inner laughter while falling
asleep one night after visiting my Buddhist teacher Zasep
Rinpoche, and realizing that it is actually possible and perhaps
preferable to 'die laughing'. A "vajra" is a Sanskrit word
meaning thunderbolt in Hindu mythology, and in Buddhism
signifies the male aspect in tantric iconography and the quality
of indestructible compassionate skillful means.)

Morning; Remorse and Revelation

I wake with the taste of anger, jealousy,
disappointment still fresh
from a meal of selfishness
I lie under clouds like skin, fibers and fat
on an earth of bone and fluid
Being a small red blood cell
myself

Untitled – at Rigdzin Ling

Manzanita
atop a slight rise
forms a natural shrine
The place a person
could place an offering
or say a prayer
The place a meditator
could sit
and become Buddha

Untitled - for Theresa

Simple is the sunlight
reflected in water
never touching
gold hidden in ore
But the fire
within....
Ah, there

Something Else

What is past is gone
What lingers melts away
When you leave – to work
I yearn to follow, to call you back
have you call in sick
and play together in this bright day

Instead I sit, body firm like a tree stump
bitter taste in my mouth
eyes and mind kept alert by the bright view
out the window

The house is still and quiet
like you've taken its heart with you
And my mind wanders and wonders
over how I came to depend on you so much
What to do next – go ski, go fix something, go study
But the effort of it all just makes me want to sleep

How did it come to have so much distance
between us
Distance replacing love
Love stretched so thin
Love once so thick like honey
now dispersed like pure air
without a trace of scent

I imagine this my Death Song
from my heart, clear and simple
to be sung over and over as I meet my end

playing like static to draw out what comes next
Instead I brush my teeth
and do
something else

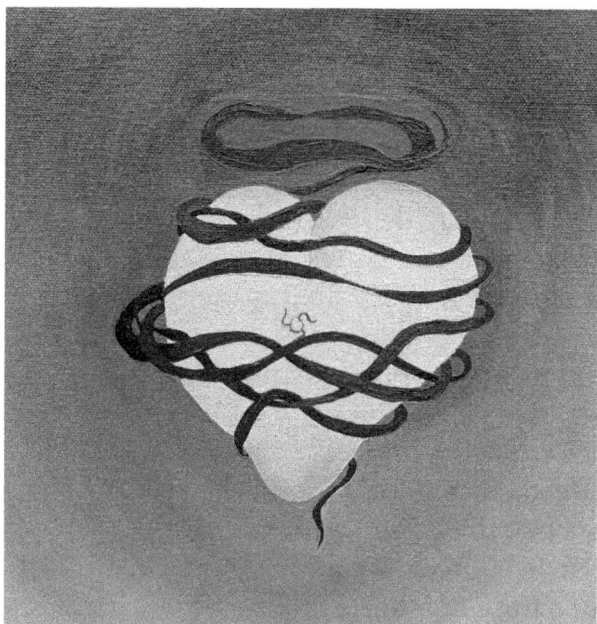

A Simple Act

For years I practiced
esoteric postures
to give me something
I thought I lacked
But when my hour
of need came
they didn't help
didn't make it through
the great ego filter
Only awareness made it
Only familiarity with that
awareness helped

Later when I was tired
and down and wondering
if I'd drown anyways
my lover gave me some advice
a simple street-wise posture
to stand firm, feet planted apart
back straight, head up

When I started by lifting my head
I realized I was only in shallow
if swiftly moving water
and I wouldn't drown
couldn't really without wanting to
as long as I kept my head up
But really the swift rapids
is less glorified than that
more of an old cup of coffee
that I make swirl if I

fiddle with enough
But if I tried I could
drown in it too
while trying hard to wake up perhaps
or just make a point
or not

Somewhere someone is making
the choice to awake
to rise
to shine
to lift their head
recall the view
Perhaps they are swimming
or sharing a hot
morning cup
Whatever it is
I'm sure it's
a simple act
of love, of faith
of recognition

For Kailash

Mind like the wind blew
Away when I let it go
The way of all things

At Tsog

In the blaze of practice
I realize Troma Nagmo is
supreme wrath
and I feel my deepest terror.
Terrified and terrible all at once
I experience the pride of the deity.

(A "tsog" is a ritual celebration feast in the Vajrayana tradition of
Tibetan Buddhism. Troma Nagmo is a particularly fierce female
deity)

Murphy

Life is but a word
for a whole
that is more vast
wonderful and terrible
than we can say

(Written at the unexpected death of a dear friend.)

Pain

Pain passes and I'm left
with myself, like bits and
pieces of memories
And it doesn't matter that
I'm closed off in a room
The whole world is here

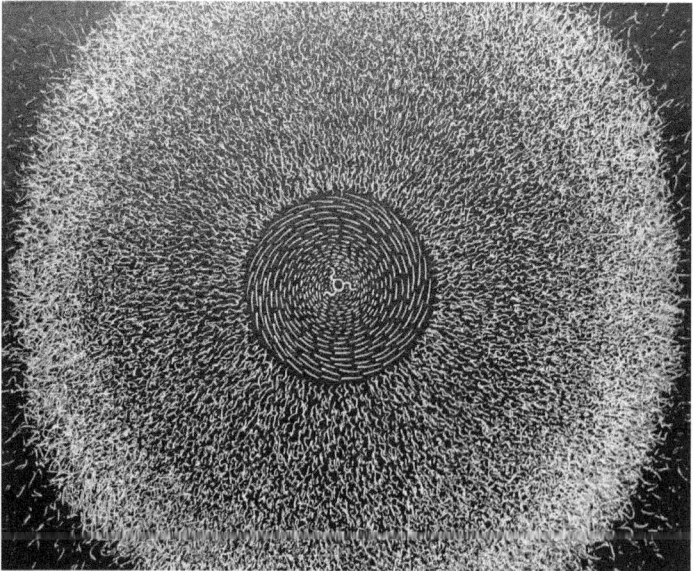

No Exit

In the middle of the night
(unable to keep still and sleep)
trying futilely to relax in the bath
(and escape these ceaseless pains of a broken back)
I ask, "What is the best way to painlessly kill myself?"
And from Carol's reaction
(sobbing at the edge of the tub)
I clearly see there is no 'painless' way
Pain is inescapable
Pain is what's left when all the band aids fall away
Pain is what floats like an oily film on the surface of
the vast ocean of experiences
The vastness which is also inescapable
So pain and vastness become the best teachers
Experiences and their true nature
Inescapable
A life of torture with no exit
Until there is acceptance

No Exit - Part 2

Fucking Fuck Fuck Fucker
Off with the leg
Pull it out by the roots
Chop it off at the hip
Cauterize it with tar
Jump off a tall cliff
with no time for goodbyes
Gladly face a firing squad
or a junkie's dose times ten
Chop my pinkie off to redirect the pain
Shoot out windows or passing cats
Hurl empty bottles at garden walls
Or bite wads of clothing, leather strapping,
handy thumbs
till the next wave passes
Or keep very still and hope and wish and pray
that somehow miraculously the pain will stop
But before it does I'm scheming of a way to kill it
And thrash and wail, moan and cry
to distract my physical torment with emotional hell
Until eventually I'm exhausted of possibilities,
of patience, of dignity
And the drugs finally start to kick in
to take the edge off slightly
enough to let me listen to what
the pain has to say
To where it can take me within
Away from ideas of escape or exit
I'm waiting....
Even without patience, I'm waiting

Living Room Floor

November light and colors stream in
through the window
and I notice it, like in the eye of a storm
A whirlwind that has included pain and creativity
but always distraction –
of strivings and graspings at
accumulation and accomplishment.
And in a moment – of sun, sound and color –
it all settles to be just this;

Everyone, everywhere burning like so many
points of light.
Like on a Christmas tree, connected by strings
amid the tinsel and baubles and
homemade ornaments of meaning.
Light that knows no division of inside or out,
me or you,
us or them.

Smoking In The Pygmy Twylyte

Life in all these moments
tumbling along, down and around
corner store and back
a pack of cigarettes and six of beer
paper bag, ripping from the strain
of gravity
of levity hidden within
a brown shopping bag
straining to carry so much
release and freedom
straining to hold it in
keep it from smashing, crashing
down on the sidewalk, into the gutter
or flying away, like released
butterflies
"Beer on the run", on wings of
smoking tobacco
The sidewalk that has seen so many
feet. Soles. Soul's soles. Soles of Souls
and peered up so many skirts
in complete disinterest
Preferring the parade of
clouds ahead
Praying for rain
to wash it's face once again
of Soul's Soles
and all the shit they carry.

Sun shining
burning through the haze
reflecting puddles

pulling them up and away
back
before they make the journey home
burning the sucker up
burning everything in it's path
The Shining Path
The mystery of light itself
illumination
reflections on the mirror of stuff
the miracle of being able to mirror
just by being
A lump to bounce off
to reflect the stuff we see
and absorb what we don't

Soul's parading under clouds over concrete
that no light can reveal
that hold no color
that mirror no nothing
unseen, unknown, unfelt, unwanted
unwelcome
cursed to just be, to witness, to move
Step in shit and walk it off
To float in the gap
between
Heaven and Hell
forever between
here and there
searching for love and acknowledgment
everywhere, anywhere
craving a glimpse
in the mirror of everything
vainly

between there and back again
home away from home
home in the heart of It
home
always here
Effortlessly floating along
the sidewalk
under twilight clouds
squinting into the sun
An imperceptible puff
and bottled intoxication
just enough to relax the tight grip
The proof that God exists
and just wants us to be happy
Everlastingly happy and free
happy and free and needing
to piss.

April's Smile

It all falls away
when you let it
go
when you stop building it
up
or holding it together.
And there is so much
encouragement to do just this
nothing.
Like the Sun effortlessly alighting
on everything
in its path;
the eager receptive quasi-smile
of a dog;
the fluid jumble of notes in a slide guitar solo.
There is really nothing to think about
that really needs being thought of.
Everything already has its
appropriate time and place,
the result of actions already taken
like that sunlight radiating out from
our Sun.

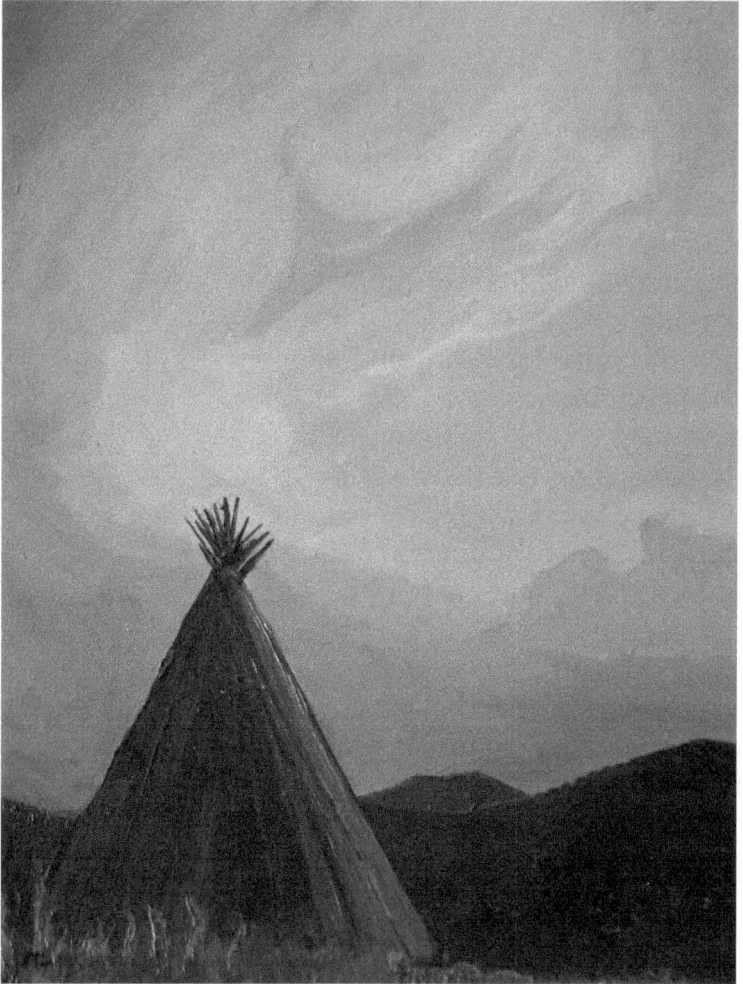

Hide and Seek

In the big picture
all that really matters is
the nonduality of everything
and the observing mind.
The fact that awareness (the light)
mind (the filter),
and everything we experience
(the particles and/or waves of stuff)
is one,
and none other than unified.
Unified primordially
and so completely
that it is more zero than one.
In the complete simplicity of this
nonduality
is wisdom and compassion;
wisdom in being just what it is
nothing more or less,
and compassion in being the perfect
expression of all causes and effects.

In the small picture
we look for meaning and contrast,
search for wisdom
and cultivate compassion,
and get lost in the surface reflections
and ripples;
lost in the experience of joy and despair,
love and hate, confusion and insight,
interest and boredom.

Lost and found, around and 'round
like a child's game
played in fun, played in terror, played in compulsion,
played in ignorance,
played with others,
played with ourselves.

The Catch 22 of it all –
the whole and the parts,
the fleeting and eternal;
the so vast I'm gone
the so personal I'm here
and enamored, enraged, engulfed, enlightened.
There is no better or less than
in this mix,
no up or down
no light or dark
no clarity or obscuration,
only what we think we know,
and what we experience when we forget
ourselves
in the joy of it all.

Map of the Human Heart

The map of the human heart
knows no boundaries
yet being a map,
being a picture,
being something we may care to refer to,
has an edge
like maps of old
where dragons dwell
before an abrupt edge
(before the infinite border)
a cascade of all accumulated contents
into the void
filled with all those contents
(the endless accumulations)
but always empty
always voiding
always waiting to absorb
everything we've ever tried to build and hold
the alpha and omega of all loss.
But my void also now has nebulas
clouds of dust from all previous culminations
clouds of potential where new stars
are birthed.

And this is just out at the edge of my map.
Within, are all the wonders of the known world
all manner of plants and animals, imagined and real
all images I've ever entertained, willingly or not
contained, collaged, collected and held
in defense of that waiting loss.
And this world of my hopes and fears

is illuminated by love - "my love", I might say
like I could say, "my world", "my Sun", "my heart"
a shared world of shared illumination
always shifting, always pulsing,
always wonderful, always terrible.

The map of the human heart is painstakingly drawn,
etched with blood, sweat and tears
in neural networks and cellular holograms.
It is beautiful in its whole
yet confusing, even overwhelming, in its parts
in its experience
in its twists and turns
convolutions, chambers, caverns
deserts, beaches, and lonely plains.
It is drawn in record of all we yearn for and want,
and all we reject and fear.
It is drawn when we know it,
and when we don't,
in our sleep and our ecstasies
our boredom and our heightened sensitivities
in our vastness and our pettiness.
It is drawn alone and together
with friends, strangers, lovers and enemies.
It is drawn around concepts,
drawn around hints of impressions
clouds of feeling
wisps of nothing we recognize
or care to acknowledge.
It is drawn simply and complexly
consciously and not.

The map of the human heart knows no boundaries,

in its essence
in its actual territory
in its living
in its changing
in its endless falling, opening, pulsing, dreaming.

It can never be drawn or seen or held
but try we do anyways...

Beyond Words – for Carol

Pastel flowers against
a sky blue ground,
a moose in a lake
amid autumnal colors
and vibrant hued waters,
a bison on a hill
a study in gentle yellow
ocher, power and peace.
Such are the pictures
around my true-love's head
as she gently sleeps or wakes
the last and first she sees each day
a reminder of the natural harmony
within and without us
the beauty of light and space.

When Is Enough?

No pain no gain
they say.
Or in my case
no pain no poetry
at least no good poetry.
Without the pain, without
the lack, without the raw
exposure
it is all just sentimental
sugar-coated approximations.

But how many moments are needed
to make a life meaningful?
How many moments of pure
appreciation
wonder
beauty
love
awareness
does it take?
Is one enough? Why not, when
one is all you ever get,
when each moment is a unique moment
and the raw essence timeless in that moment.

What does it take to be able to say, I lived enough,
I loved enough,
I gave enough,
I served enough,
I appreciated it all enough?
How can there be an end, a completion, a fullness?

How can there be a liberation without the suffering of
karma, or acceptance without rejection and struggle?

And so it flows, ebbs and flows, endlessly
within and without us
Without the play of these opposites we'd
surely grow soft, dull, complacent
and eventually fall asleep.... the illusion of death
masquerading as an endless sleep.
But that implies we wouldn't keep dreaming.

The Discovery Of This

What is love
but a vortex
of lust and belonging
doubt, suspicion and fear
that pulls us in
and down
and under
and drags us along the
bottom
before
spitting us out
the other side
out onto the grass
of a shore
beyond
all this we bring
turned and twisted
spun and rinsed
washed
and cleansed
and made whole
by what it is
we never knew we had
what propelled and impelled
what waited and watched
what rested and delivered
what we never knew we wanted
what we never knew was ours.
What is love
but the discovery
of this.

For Shae

Padmasambhava comes riding
and demons run for cover
flushed out by
the all seeing eye of
Sun-like awareness.

Padmasambhava comes riding
up the steep cliff
one bolt at a time
move by move
till there is nothing left to do.

Padmasambhava comes riding
lasso in hand
snagging ego as it makes its stand
proud or pitiful
it makes no difference once caught.

Padmasambhava comes riding
singing, laughing, joyous dancing
lifting up and cutting through
simultaneously
in one swift motion.

Padmasambhava comes riding
revealing all to be but a dream
an illusion, dew drop, mirage
of the mind
merciless in his all encompassing view

(Padmasambhava, credited with establishing the Buddhism of India in the wilds of 8th century Tibet, symbolizes the enlightened activity of compassionate wisdom that both blesses and removes obstacles. This poem was in response to my daughter Shae having some difficulties on a local rock climb called "Padmasambhava Comes Riding.")

Remembering Yak Peak

Mountain stream flows
Wine flows
Music flows
Rocks rise and crumble
simultaneously,
the essence
of life and creativity
the joy of just being
moving steadily up
over clean inviting granite
in opposition to gravity
in balance to its inexorable force
rising through a mix of sheer will
and resulting bliss.

Climbing
as the perfect metaphor
for it all;
camaraderie, isolation, focus, individual risk
and accomplishment,
shared but separate.
Meditation in motion
communion with the ordinary
sublimity in the most basic
space and rock, effort, resolve and release.
While clouds and large birds
float overhead....
Effortlessly.

Stumbling To Manifestation

Passion for Life
- for living
for doing whatever
weird thing we love to do -
gives so much.

What else really is there
worth living for?
(Duty, obligation, expectation...?
surly these ideals are no
match to joy and enthusiasm.)

Yet children give up joy so readily
for maturity, respectability, and responsibility,
a cage of safe conventions
and then yearn for those days of
innocence and abandon.

Somehow passion survives this
distorting process
in whatever weird way it can - and does
against reason
against caution
against restraint
against the advice of others, who can never
know what is in one's own heart.

Awareness

Awareness centered
In a room of mirrors each
Reflecting just that

Little Things

Little things
it's the little things that make up the bulk of life
even the big things
have lots of little things around them
and it's the little things
that we actually do and see and hear, taste, feel, smell
and know,
little things we share
or little things we enjoy in private
little things we remember or look forward to
little things we sometimes only miss when we notice
other little things
in an ocean of
little things.

What We Resist, Persists

Grasp and hold (label and record)
moment after moment
day after day
year after year
from cradle to grave
driven by instinct
refined by learning
our deepest habit; the reification of self
the clinging to order
- a life ring in an ocean of chaos.
Grasp and hold, label and name,
moments of endless waves seen as
the particles we know,
in vain.

Peace, beauty, release, bliss, love
exist beneath all we think or desire,
beneath all we fear
that we feel beneath all we grasp and hold.
Fear that we feel
beneath the order that we grasp and hold.
Grasp and hold (label and record)
Fear that we feel
when we meet the chaos
in this moment - each moment
free of order
free of labels
free of reference
free of hope
free of boundaries, or limits, or restraints
on our habits, and the fears that fuel them.

The desire to be,
to escape our own face
the watchful gaze
of passionless awareness.
That which exists before the world was made.
That which exists when all worlds end.
That which exists now and only now,
in this moment, here
in this space that is spaceless spaciousness itself,
beneath any place we know and would call home,
beneath any story we would tell and call our own,
beneath all we grasp and hold
to seek comfort in;
Refuge
within the transparent
ephemeral
imaginary
bubble of our mind
the line we place around
all we grasp and hold (label and record)...

As Simple As That!

To be or not to be
is NOT the question.
It is the quest,
and a vain one at that!

To do is the fact of Life
that is beyond question
(and so beyond needing an answer).

To do is all we ever can do,
all that Life can do, has done, will do.
And doing is always a verb.
Nouns are the illusion.

So we do, and create illusions,
habitually
Or at least I have.

So we do, and undo illusions,
diligently
Or at least I have.

So we do, and don't do illusions,
effortlessly
Or at least I have.

And that's about the limit of my knowledge.

As simple as that!

Fixin' To Die

Sometimes
I urge to throw myself off a cliff
knowing I'll fall like a rock
"Thud!" to the ground.
But what is this urge, this thought, this fantasy?
Is it the urge to fly
or die?
Is it the desire to be free
or simply cease to be?

Or is it just another urge to do,
and ponder the consequences
of this doing?
Another act in an endless
ocean of action.
Another moment of awareness
and the reminder that real freedom
is more about freedom from desire,
than freedom to have
- things, civil rights, spiritual powers -
or to act on impulses.

Sometimes it's just good to know
a little of what lurks beneath
the surface.
And that in one way or another
we're all just
fixin' to die.

The Mind

The mind
is a terrible thing to waste they say,
but what about to just have?!
It is terrible
to watch and experience, for sure;
a web of patterned beauty
designed to snare and feed,
a fiber, resilient
but without real connectivity,
an illusion of an illusion builder
the insubstantial thoughts that the solidity
of apparent reality rest upon,
a mirage inhabited by
imaginary beings...

No wonder anxiety is common.
It is nothing if not a sane
reaction to such unsubstantiated is-ness.
Sanity experienced as madness,
such is the irony when one sees the
complete insubstantiality of mind,
and the objects of mind
mere imputations of self and other.

From within the web and static buzz and
cage-like trap of the mind
such impressions are heresy, fantasy, lunacy.
But from outside the mind,
outside the localizing, ordering construct of thought
such impressions are obvious
and common place.

The sages aren't wise (with accumulated knowledge)
as much as accurate in their descriptions
of what simply happens
without any way to pin it down
and say what it is.
And yet, this simple clarity IS wisdom.

"Your Mind - You're Just Imagining It."
is more than a clever bumper sticker.
It is the essence being pointed out
in yet again an obvious way,
pointing out that the terribleness of
wasting a mind is simply in not appreciating
the play it spins
for our entertainment and entrapment,
and thus the recognition, or at least intimation,
of all that lies beyond it,
off the stage, out of the spotlight
without a script or actor
or even audience.

What is freedom without the experience of restraint?
What is liberty without a knowledge of servitude?
What is love without a taste of fear,
or music without the contrast of silence or chaos?

What is illusion without the mind?

Dreams

Life is a dream within a dream
and on, etc. etc.
Layers and layers of moments
deposited like sediment
With all the attendant metaphors
of geology we can imagine
fossilization, petrification, metamorphic processes.
But what is it really?
What is it beyond sound and vision
vibration and light?
What is it outside the world, the universe,
the dreams of our conceptualizing mind?
As Lao Tzu said awhile back,
Darkness within darkness
The gate to all mysteries...

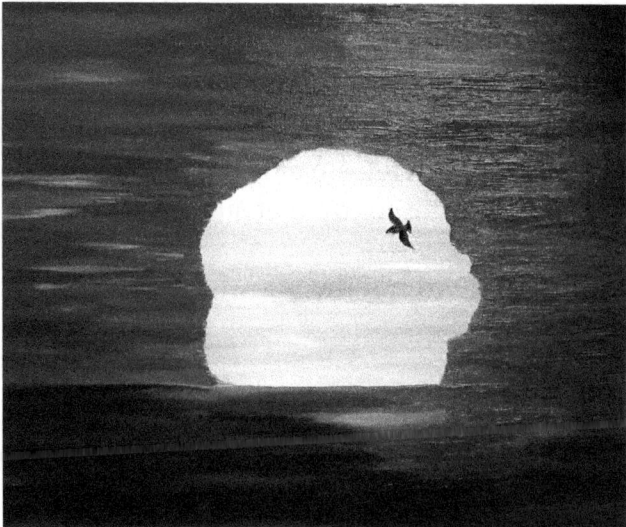

Hardwired

Listening to Lucinda in the cold clear mornings
Reading Conrad late into the nights
Basking in the glow revealed
down where the spirit meets the bone and the
heart of darkness waits close, eternal, timeless, fresh
as winter sets in and attention turns inward
laboring to take measure of another year
another year of separating the wheat from the chaff
(like the 7th century monk Shen Hsiu earnestly
polishing his mind's mirror)
the essential from the debris
of each experience...

But how can any of it be inessential
in the balance of things?

The glow says gently, says warmly, says blissfully
It is ALL fuel for the fire
Nothing can be outside this play of light and shadow
Nothing is shallow
Nothing is deep
Everything here and now is alive
even the echoes
and shimmering mirages
of the endless words in our little thought bubbles.

We come into Life fully loaded with an
ocean of habits and conceptions
bursting to project another world onto this one
an order on the chaos our senses sift

We come yearning to be normal and make it all so
make it all conform to expectations, ours and others
with a genetic need to have it all be safe and sane
Hardwired to make sense of it all.

But to break out of this childish need to conform
to this conspiracy of relatives
(All Our Relations - from worm to whale)
requires more than we can imagine.
A most unnatural leap,
the essence of faith - into the unknown.
A leap beyond
rejecting all desire
to feed our selves,
or grasping at all
we desire in an endless loop.
A leap beyond with no reason
for no reason
but to be
free.

Within The Fog of Awakening

...Go high with that
glimpsed snow-capped peaks
beyond forested hills
under clear blue skies

Many miles to go before I wake...

Go home with that
enveloping caress of
soft painted lips and
sweet fragrant skin

Many smiles to go before I sleep...

Go down with that
all the way down
through twilight tunnels
and out the other side

This labyrinth of dreams
both waking, sleeping and in between
exhausts any clear notion of
separation, destination, or goal

The Illusion of I

No matter how good or bad it may seem
how high we fly or low we fall
we really aren't who we think we are
merely the aggregate of all we do
really just a verb and not a noun
not even a mote of dust drifting
or bit of flotsam floating
simply the act of drifting or floating itself.
self-aware motion at best, but not much more.

And as everyone with a body knows
(and isn't that everyone?)
not only does our form constantly change
but it doesn't ever make it through
the portal of death.
Only awareness, the most basic,
most sublime moment we can know ever survives.

Yet this indefinable, ineffable awareness
in all its limitless compassion is
the perfect sponge for all our habits
the perfect mirror for all our projections
the perfect vehicle for all our dreams
best embodied in the wisdom of insecurity
that nagging persistent intuition of the illusion of I

Can you imagine how beautiful life would be
if no one suffered this illusion?
As Alan Watts once so clearly put it,
"Free from clutching at themselves
the hands can handle;

free from looking at themselves
the eyes can see;
free from trying to understand itself
thought can think."

What more is there to say?
Free from trying to describe it
silence arises as a complete sentence.

The Heart of It

Nietzsche said,
"If you wish to strive for peace of soul and pleasure,
then believe.
If you wish to be a devotee of truth,
then inquire."
So what is found in belief? Whatever you want.
And what is found through inquiry? What is.

Form is Emptiness. Emptiness is Form.
Or so the sutras say.
And yet this isn't just some erudite way to express
the simple truth everyone knows
that opposites always exist together
and are only meaningful in contrast to each other
like love and fear, hot and cold, high and low,
light and dark
so clearly expressed in the swirling
interdependent binary drops of yin and yang.

No, form and emptiness aren't opposites
they aren't even two halves of a whole
or two truths (although some call them that)
or just two ways of seeing a unity.
They are simply two words for the same thing
- like far and distant.
A reminder that we can't have one without the other
that everything is merely an appearance,
and that all appearance is simply the expression of
emptiness.

Or to put it more poetically;

that everything is the display of Dharmakaya
("Truth Body")
which is perhaps the closest term Buddhists have to
the monotheistic concept of God.
So there is nothing that isn't
the direct expression of this
Emptiness/Dharmakaya/God.
Not that the stuff of everyday life is the creation
or product, residue or echo of these
intangibly great ineffable concepts
but that it is none other than
Emptiness/Dharmakaya/God.
And thus all we experience is this - directly.
And no matter –
when the bubble of ego/ignorance arises
(samsara)
this Dharmakaya/God isn't diminished.
And when the bubble of ego/ignorance dissolves
(nirvana)
this Dharmakaya/God isn't improved.
The nature of this Dharmakaya/God is unchanging.
And, most essentially,
the nature of it and its appearance is an illusion.

As some great sage long ago once sang;
'Row, row, row your boat gently down the stream.
Merrily, merrily, merrily, merrily life is but a dream.'
A dream which embodies perfect compassion
in all moments
Yet all too often is experienced as merely
the confusing currents of our individual passions.

Or to put it even more simply;

It is all light.
Light that is self-cognizant awareness itself
complete in all qualities
condensed through the filters of our little mind
refracted through the prisms of our experience
reified through the projections of our ego.
And so, instead of recognizing it
as simply this self-aware nature of light
we mistakenly interpret it as OUR self
and impose a dualistic world of self and other
on everything.

Or simpler yet;
It is all, and only can be, a verb
a doing of Life itself, which we call living
And any nouns we perceive are just
a frozen moment of this.

Only this...
doing, doing, doing
this Life, this Awareness, this Truth Body
not found to be anything, or truly existent anywhere
not found to be other than its radiant
playful appearance
not found within or outside these mere labels
of designation
How can it be otherwise?
How can there be anything else?
How can we grasp what isn't even there?!

Two Word Poet

Ah, so

Postscript

The Nine Lives of Pluto Cat

Prologue

In the spring of 1982 our blond cat "Larch", who not only glowed at night, but also lacking claws, testicles and any farm sense, had lasted less than a month at our new raw-land homestead (but, oh was he blissed-out for that brief month, his first away from city streets). We were pretty sure it had been an owl that took him, but it could just as easily have been a Red Tailed Hawk or Golden Eagle. Thinking we needed a companion for our young black lab Moonshadow, and a mouser for our rustic tent camp, we quickly found a replacement in the form of a tiny, all black, male kitten who we named "Pluto".

Pluto-cat came from hardy local mountain stock, and so we felt we had made a good start in our effort to establish a family and alternative way of life in the hills of North Eastern Washington. We were young, my partner and I, fresh out of college, idealistic and enthusiastic to get back to the land, and so the notion of building our mountain home with a new kitten seemed appropriate enough. What we didn't know at the time was how much of a survivor Pluto would turn out to be, and what he would manage to teach us in the process of shedding his many lives.

Life 1 – Kitten

Pluto was quickly at home in our tent camp. It was

early spring in the mountains, still cold and sometimes snowy. Pluto loved to nestle into our down sleeping bags, and spend his days hiding and playing under the old canvas tarp-tent with makeshift visqueen walls. He was a sweet little thing, full of joy and mischief, and he delighted us, even though he would occasionally poop in the middle of the sleeping bags...

As Pluto grew older he showed a remarkable confidence, loyalty and independence. He'd sit for hours and watch us build our home, and come hiking with us as we explored the surrounding hills on days off, often traveling more than a few miles with us.

Life 2 – Young Tom – A'wandering

Eventually as a young tom Pluto took off and spent what seemed like months during the next spring and summer out alone chasing mysterious tail. We never saw him during this time until he limped home one day all torn up. His ears where cut, face scratched, and hair matted, but what was most alarming was his arm. He had been cut up fighting and the skin of his right arm was punctured, encrusted and oozing yellow puss from several small holes. He stunk, and didn't look so good.

I took tinctures of Calendula and Hypercium, and poured them into his wounds, covered them with some gauze, and then wrapped his whole arm in a cast of athletic tape. For a couple of weeks he hobbled around, staying close to home, enjoying what attention we lavished upon him. When I finally cut the bandages away his whole arm was fresh and pink and hairless, and he apparently had no infection. He was healthy and rejuvenated, and he was also completely different in temperament.

Life 3 – Return of the Prodigal Son

So, Pluto was reborn a renewed cat, still a tom, but mellower, and never to wander as much again. He was clearly appreciative of the nursing we had provided, and he showed this by again following us closely on our daily walks along the ridges and forest trails of our mountain home. He also brought us various offerings including some very beautiful birds, like the Lazuli Bunting, Mountain Bluebird, Western Tanager, Ruby-crowned Kinglet, Evening and Pine Grosbeaks, as well as an assortment of rodents like field mice, voles, chipmunks and once, one late summer evening, a flying squirrel - carried alive through an open window and then released to find it's own way out through the open door in three soaring leaps!

During this time we decided to discourage his relentless (and highly effective) hunting of birds by putting a little bell on his neck. I will never forget the look on his face when I placed the collar on him and told him earnestly that he was not going to kill the birds anymore. He looked at me with a mix of shocked alarm and hurt, and then suddenly, furiously, turned his head to stare close into the wall for what seemed like hours.

Life 4 – Jealous Bastard

Pluto was now well on his way to satisfactory domestication, but he still had a few odd and obnoxious habits. One was he would still sometimes shit on the soft downy comforter bedding (never knowing what a litter box or indoor toilet was he took it upon himself to sometimes improvise). Another was he felt the need to claim his territory by marking his scent up and down the walls and furniture. And, he appeared to be jealous.

Once he woke my partner up in the middle of the night by spraying her in the face. It was winter, and I took some small pleasure in simply opening the second floor window and placing him vertically on the log wall exterior. As we lay there wondering what had just happened and trying to calm down we could hear him slowly sliding, trying desperately to continue to hang on, and eventually fall with a thud into the snowy flower garden below.

After this we began to put him out at night, but still had to endure him climbing up the corner of the house and onto the roof to perch on the skylight directly above the bed and watch us (actually more like glare) as the snow fell on him in the sub-zero dark.

So, he became an outdoor cat again, and we settled into an uneasy truce. We'd let him come in when we were there, and let him stay in as long as he didn't mark up the house. But each night we'd put him out to resume his exposed, and only slightly warm perch on the skylight where he'd scowl down on us in exile.

Life 5 – Sick and Left to Die

As Pluto grew older and more headstrong (and less welcome in our family) he also eventually became sick. For weeks he appeared to be having trouble urinating. He'd walk around clearly agitated and unable to release more than a dribble, then only a few drops at a time, and finally none at all, even though he frequently tried. We were devout (if not very compassionate) Buddhists in those days, and so had the dilemma of not liking him, but not being able to kill him outright. I remember saying, "If he survives the night we'll take him to the vet."

In the morning he surprised us by limping up to the house, and so we drove him the 40 miles in to see the vet. The vet couldn't believe we had neglected him so badly for so long. I looked at her and flatly said, "We wanted him to die."

Dr. June proceeded to inform us that Pluto had a bladder infection probably caused by not getting enough water and having too much salt in his cheap cat food diet. Then without delay or any anesthetic, as we stood watching, she snipped off the tip of his penis with scissors, stuck a wire into him and routed out his plugged urethra. His distended bladder immediately emptied onto the steel operating table. He must have been holding more than a pint of urine. She kept him for the night to see if he'd survive with antibiotic treatment, and when we returned the next day she sent us off with several large bottles of saline solution, a large hypodermic needle, and instructions to keep him hydrated with regular injections. During his stay with the good doctor Pluto had also had his testicles removed. It had been a difficult time for him, no doubt.

The horror and enormity of what we had helped create for Pluto became clear for us once we got him home. For the next week he was very weak and unable to eat, drink or walk. Somehow his back legs were now paralyzed from uremic poisoning and without the ability to control his bladder he would simply drag himself around the floor leaking out whatever fluids we injected him with, leaving a wide wet swath in his wake.

We babied him with guilty, loving care. Now we actually worried about him, and were very happy when we woke one morning to find two little dead mice waiting for us at the bottom of the ladder to the sleeping loft. We knew he'd survive and recover.

Life 6 – A Gentler Kinder Fat Cat

After that ordeal of neglect, callousness and contrition, amazingly Pluto was thankful. Once again he was reborn a completely different cat. He healed quickly, returned to our heart's affection, and became a full and welcome member of the family again. Once again he'd take long walks with us, watch closely as we worked in the garden and orchard, and even travel long distance with us – once spending a week on the road living out of a small Subaru Wagon with me and our two dogs, taking regular leashed walks in city parks and highway rest stops, and never once making a mess in the car.

Years passed and my life changed. My original partner moved away. The two dogs did as well. Pluto and I remained behind on the mountain, somewhat of an odd couple. No longer young and adventurous he preferred to stay home and get fat. In fact it seemed that for a while his only passion was to eat, and with his eating disorder he became huge. He had reached middle age.

Before too long I met a new lady friend and invited her to move in along with her two young daughters. We eventually got married, got new dogs, and made a daughter of our own. Pluto took it all in stride, and was relatively tolerant of the girls, their expectations of him to sometimes play dress-up, and the addition of several more cats to the household. Life was good, well, usually.

It was also during this time that I had the rare treat of experiencing the full display of his affection for me. One day I was sitting at the kitchen table with him. He was in front of me, close and probably drooling from his nose as he tried to rub against me, suddenly he reached out and grabbed my face in both paws, with claws extended and firmly imbedded in my cheeks, while he also bit down on the tip of my nose. He held me helpless like that for what seemed like minutes, as he stared into my eyes and purred. Later someone told me that was the equivalent of a French kiss from a cat.

Life 7 – Finally Domesticated, Kind Of...

But as affectionate and passionate as Pluto obviously was he was also still a cat and sometimes acted out his jealousy and selfishness. In fact he was steadily becoming ornery in his old age. When he once in a fit slashed the cheek of my younger step-daughter (then maybe about 6 years old) I decided he was too dangerous to keep (probably if truth be told, more concerned for the safety of our new born girl). I gathered an old burlap sack, some string and a large rock and took him to the car.

I had stopped being a devout and orthodox Buddhist by then, and so had no vows, nor ethical restraints to keep me from killing him directly. I had every intention to do just that by putting him into the bag with the rock, tying it up and throwing him off a bridge into a particularly deep spot in the river where he'd never be found. As we sat in the car, he on the passenger seat beside me, I told him of my plan, and his fate. He looked at me with panic in his eyes.

We sat there looking at each other for several minutes in silence. I had every intention of murdering him, and yet... And yet, he was my oldest companion, maybe even friend. Over the years I had even come to see him as perhaps the reincarnation of an old lover, who in his own peculiar way had shown his dedication and fierce love. The moment passed and I told him I couldn't drown him, and that he'd better get it together and change his ways. And he did, like he had done many times before, again as if turning over a new leaf, instantly transforming into a completely different personality.

Life 8 – Old and Left to Die Part 2

Pluto lived for a couple of more years as the gentle and mellow senior patriarch of the household. When he eventually became blind it was in the late winter of 1998. He was almost 16 years old. He was clearly dying a natural death, and we decided out of respect to let him do it on his own terms. He wandered off one last time alone, in a mix of walking, crawling and tumbling westward down the hillside through the deep snow into the night... We said our goodbyes as we watched him go, but he was clearly preoccupied.

The next day we were surprised by the visit of a well meaning Good Christian neighbor who showed up carrying Pluto. She had found him lying in the ditch along the county road, where he had tumbled, almost dead from exposure, and thought we'd want him back home. We thanked her, not wanting to tell her she had foiled our plans for a peaceful natural death for the old guy.

For the next week Pluto stayed in a wire rabbit cage in the living room, unable to control his bladder, eat, see or apparently sleep. All he wanted to do was get out, and so continually spent his days pacing in circles, literally crawling up the walls and bashing his face against the wires trying to walk off again into the sunset.

It was pitiful for all of us.

Life 9 – Prolonged by Good Intentions, Released by Kindness

I had to travel to Seattle to do some construction work for a friend, so I missed what happened next. My wife told me the story, and it somehow remains vivid for me as if I had been there at the time.

It was a crisp and cold March morning when she had called our neighbor Ron to bring his .22 rifle and help put Pluto down. They stood in the driveway, with the girls inside, perhaps unaware of what was going to happen, and shot the blind old wretched cat.

The story goes that in a brilliant flash the air became crystal clear, pristine, still, and almost brittle. It was like the limpid clarity behind this world of appearances was revealed. In that moment they both felt an unexpected sense of awe and simplicity and calm. They stood there in that transformed space and hugged each other and cried. In an instant Pluto was gone, and in the release, something remarkable had been revealed.

Later when I heard this story it reminded me of the experience devotees of accomplished meditation masters sometimes witness when their teacher drops their body and merges their mind with the Clear Light. It made me wonder (in more than one sense of the word) if Pluto was not in fact a great bodhisattva here to teach us a lesson or two.

After Life – An Epilogue

It has been many years since these incidences of Pluto's life occurred, yet as I recall them now they bring back strong emotions. Especially remembering the time I almost drowned him, sitting in the car together as we pondered his fate and our connection, it makes my heart completely open, and I find the tears just pouring from my eyes.

Pluto was more than a cat or companion for those years. He was a glimpse of all of Life. A glimpse of the up close and personal and of the farther reaches, the extremes of what we can all experience, that are both immediate and tangible, yet also beyond the visible.

In the end it seems he was named perfectly.

About the Author

James Moore was born in 1958 to a British mother and American father just a few miles north of the equator in Central Sumatra, Indonesia, and spent most of his youth living in North America, moving steadily westward. By the time he had finished getting a degree (in Environmental Studies from Huxley College at WWU) he was ready to begin his real education homesteading in the remote hills of North Central Washington within a mile of the Canadian border. Many years later he came to settle not far away in the big city of Tonasket (population 1,020) in the beautiful Okanogan Valley, with his even more beautiful wife Carol, and their 3 dogs and 2 cats. He currently divides his time between rock climbing and hiking, oil painting, building, orcharding, gardening and playing with his pug Pema.

www.ingramcontent.com/pod-product-compliance
Lightning Source LLC
Chambersburg PA
CBHW061154040426
42445CB00013B/1681